BEARING WITNESS

GENOCIDE AND ETHNIC CLEANSING™

THE DESTRUCTION OF THE INCA CIVILIZATION

ALEXIS BURLING

Rosen YA™

Published in 2018 by The Rosen Publishing Group, Inc.
29 East 21st Street, New York, NY 10010

First Edition

Library of Congress Cataloging-in-Publication Data

Names: Burling, Alexis, author.
Title: The destruction of the Inca civilization / Alexis Burling.
Description: New York : Rosen Publishing, 2018 | Series: Bearing witness : genocide and ethnic cleansing | Includes bibliographical references and index. | Audience: Grades 7–12.
Identifiers: LCCN 2017013194 | ISBN 9781508177388 (library bound) | ISBN 9781508178699 (paperback)
Subjects: LCSH: Peru—History—Conquest, 1522–1548—Juvenile literature. | Incas—History—Juvenile literature.
Classification: LCC F3429 .B863 2018 | DDC 985/.019—dc23
LC record available at https://lccn.loc.gov/2017013194

Manufactured in the United States of America

On the cover: John Everett Millais painted *Pizarro Seizing the Inca of Peru* in 1846. It shows the Inca leader Atahualpa being ambushed by the Spanish conquistador Francisco Pizarro and his men.

CONTENTS

INTRODUCTION

In the summer of 1911, a North American explorer by the name of Hiram Bingham III was conducting research in the Andes Mountains in South America. He was searching for the fabled "lost city" of the Inca civilization, one of the most advanced cultures in the history of the Americas. His grueling expedition lasted many days, up a mountain that jutted 8,000 feet (2,438 meters) into the air. Then on July 24, accompanied by a local guide and a Peruvian policeman, he stumbled upon something astonishing.

Today, more than one million tourists visit the ruins of Machu Picchu every year. But in the fifteenth century, this majestic city was a sacred religious site for Inca leaders.

"Suddenly we found ourselves in the midst of a jungle-covered maze of small and large walls, the ruins of buildings made of blocks of white granite, most carefully cut and beautifully fitted together without cement," he wrote in *Harpers Monthly* in April 1913. "Surprise followed surprise until there came the realization that we were in the midst of as wonderful ruins as any ever found in Peru."

Bingham had originally hoped to find Vilcabamba—one of the last Inca strongholds before the civilization crumbled in the 1570s. Instead, he had rediscovered the ruins of Machu Picchu, a majestic and sacred Inca city that had remained hidden from most of the outside world for centuries.

Machu Picchu was the Inca's crown jewel, with its terraced gardens, irrigation systems, and impressive buildings built into the landscape. But it wasn't their only city. In fact, at the civilization's peak in the late fifteenth and early sixteenth centuries, Inca territory stretched nearly 2,500 miles (4,024 kilometers), from the northern border of Ecuador to the Maule River in central Chile. During this heyday, the Inca people accomplished magnificent feats in agriculture, architecture, and the construction of roads. Theirs was the largest and most powerful pre-Columbian empire in the New World, with more than ten million members who spoke at least twenty different languages.

But for a people who had dominated this part of the world since the twelfth century, the demise of their culture was swift and brutal. In a matter of hours, thousands of Inca people were slaughtered by a small army of conquistadors led by Francisco Pizarro. Pizarro was a Spanish adventurer who wanted to colonize the area and reap the benefits of the region. Atahualpa, the Inca ruler, was deposed and later executed. Within a relatively short period, the Spanish systematically conquered and subjugated the rest of the Inca people through forced labor practices and mandatory religious conversion. They killed anyone who did not cooperate.

By modern standards, the downfall of the Inca civilization could be defined as genocide—the methodical and deliberate destruction of a racial, political, or cultural group. The Spanish desired the Inca's gold and land. Because of their prejudice, the Spanish had no reservations about using violent means to get what they wanted. They used sophisticated weapons and tried to remove any trace of the Inca and their culture—their religious beliefs and cultural traditions, even the languages they spoke—from the planet. Disease and famine took care of the rest.

As with other horrific points in history, such as the murder of millions of Jews during World War II or the ethnic cleansing that took place during the Syrian Civil War, there are lessons to be learned from this tragedy. Thankfully, Inca practices and traditions have started to make a comeback in recent decades. More than one million tourists flock to Machu Picchu every year to learn about and pay homage to the ancient culture. It is a civilization that should not be forgotten.

CHAPTER 1

MIGHTY TAWANTISUYU

The history of the Inca civilization is long and complicated. It is full of conquests between tribes, ongoing familial rivalries, and squabbles over the control of natural resources. But it's also the story of the rise—and fall—of one of the most prolific and artistic cultures to ever exist.

Although written records from this ancient world are scarce (in that area at that time, history was passed down orally), it is believed that the Inca first appeared in what is now southeastern Peru around the twelfth century CE. They moved from village to village in search of enough usable land to sustain themselves. Sometime between 1150 and 1300, they settled in a fertile valley surrounded by the Andes Mountains.

What began as a series of isolated nomadic tribes soon blossomed into a small, interconnected kingdom. In some cases, the Inca struck up marriage alliances with leaders from surrounding villages to acquire more land. In others, ethnic factions fought each other for control. Land and valuable resources were seized by the victors—usually the Inca—in battle. The burgeoning city of Cusco became the center of Inca government and commerce and the capital of the region.

AN EMPIRE IS BORN

Beginning in the early 1400s, the society that was quickly becoming a full-blown Incan empire expanded into lands well outside the Cusco Valley. In 1438, Cusi Inca Yupanqui, who called himself Pachacuti, became the ninth emperor of the region. After a series of brutal skirmishes with various ethnic groups, such as the Quechua, the Chimú, and the Chanca, Pachacuti reorganized his kingdom into the Tawantinsuyu, or "Realm of the Four Parts." It featured four provincial governments run by powerful leaders. The territory located to the northwest of Cusco was named Chinchasuyu; Antisuyu was to the northeast; Contisuyu was to the southwest; and Collasuyu was to the southeast. The center of command was still located in Cusco, with the emperor at its head.

Under Pachacuti, Cusco was rebuilt into a majestic capital. Sacsahuamán, the huge fortress overlooking the city, was enlarged to a formidable size. Rivers were channeled and irrigated terraces were constructed out of the valley's verdant, hilly landscape so that large swaths of corn and more than seventy other vegetable varieties could be planted. The crops were then stored to provide sustenance for the Inca people. A state religion was created based on the worship of a god named Viracocha, and temples for worshipers were built throughout the empire.

Sacsahuamán was an Inca citadel that sat high on a hill overlooking Cusco. Today, the historic ruins are a UNESCO World Heritage Site. They are visited by thousands of tourists each year.

Pachacuti was a relatively tolerant leader, embracing ethnic diversity and allowing his subjects to practice their own religions and traditions. Still, he never lost sight of his goal to acquire more territory. He conquered smaller tribes in southern Peru and expanded his reign farther north. After Pachacuti died, his son Túpac Inca followed in his father's footsteps and seized even more land, including the Kingdom of Chimor—the Inca's only serious rival for the coast of Peru. By the time of Túpac's death in 1493, the Inca Empire stretched far north into modern-day Ecuador and Colombia.

The Inca used *quipu* to keep track of things like taxes, crops, and how many married and unmarried men and women lived in a village.

ASTONISHING ACHIEVEMENTS

At the start of the sixteenth century, the Inca Empire was vast and powerful. The Inca people made their homes in the coastal desert, the high mountains, and low-lying jungles throughout most of modern-day Peru, parts of Ecuador and Bolivia, northwest Argentina, and a large portion of Chile.

As a culture, the Inca were extraordinarily advanced and efficient. They constructed cities to suit their location, using only locally sourced materials. A typical coastal dwelling was made with adobe walls and a flat roof, while highland buildings contained intricately laid stonework that was so expertly cut and polished it didn't need mortar to stay together.

The Inca didn't maintain written records. But they devised a sophisticated method for keeping track of their supplies

PERUVIAN TEXTILES

In addition to being industrious, the Inca were also talented artists. They created ceramic bowls, pots, and vases without using a wheel. But the ancient Peruvians were best known for their textiles.

Traditional weaving, spinning, and embroidering were arts practiced by all Inca women. They made blankets, tablecloths, and rugs for their homes and clothes for their families. Woven goods were traded and sometimes used as a form of tax payment to the government.

Most Inca textiles were made using a backstrap loom—a tool that consisted of two wooden bars with a series of yarns, called the warp, stretched between them. The loom, hooked to some sort of support on one end, was then tied around a weaver's back using a strap. This kept the warp taught so the weaver could pass a different piece of yarn, called the weft, over and under to create a pattern.

Most Peruvian textiles were intricately designed. Many told stories about a significant historical event or paid homage to a particular god or goddess. Often the blankets and cloths were so well made that the Inca wrapped their dead in them to prepare the soul for its journey to the afterlife.

using a counting device called a *quipu*. It was a series of knotted strings of various thicknesses and colors that hung vertically off of a thick rope. By taking note of the color of the string or where each knot was placed on the quipu, the Inca could tell, for example, how many llamas, alpacas, or other livestock they had at their disposal. They also used the quipu to recount folk stories and the traditional poetry of their ancestors.

The most groundbreaking Inca accomplishment was perhaps their mass construction of roads. They built the most extensive and advanced network of its time, stretching nearly 25,000 miles (40,234 km) to previously unreachable territories. The eastern route ran from Quito, Ecuador, to Mendoza, Argentina. The western route followed the coastal plains. More than twenty routes crisscrossed over the western mountains, while others navigated the lowlands. Some roads even provided access to areas 16,000 feet (4,877 m) above sea level.

This ancient Inca highway is hidden within the Andes Mountains in Peru. The road stretched from the forest floor to Machu Picchu.

This interconnected highway system enabled the creation of more than two thousand provincial administrative and commercial centers, as well as frontier military forts throughout the region. These village outposts kept the empire robust and strong, but, unfortunately, not strong enough. By the 1520s, the cracks in almighty Tawantinsuyu had begun to show.

ON SHAKY GROUND

As late as 1527, the Inca Empire was a still a mostly cohesive unit ruled by the eleventh emperor, Huayna Capac. But over the next five years, a series of catastrophic events occurred that shook the very foundation of everything the Inca had tried so hard to build.

First, deadly diseases swept across the continent. Searching for land and wealth, European prospectors entered what are now Panama and Colombia in the late fifteenth and early sixteenth centuries. They brought with them illnesses like smallpox and influenza. The diseases spread quickly. Having never encountered such epidemics before, the Inca and other indigenous peoples had no way of preventing, fighting, or treating them. Estimates for the number of Inca people who died from European-borne diseases range from two-thirds to 95 percent.

Secondly, Huayna Capac and his eldest son and heir Ninan Cuyuchi died from smallpox in 1527. Two of Huayna's remaining sons, Atahualpa and his half-brother Huáscar, began fighting over who would control the empire. Atahualpa

This fifteenth-century portrait is of Huayna Capac, the eleventh Sapa Inca of the Inca Empire. He lived from 1464 to 1527.

garnered the support of Quito and the northern part of the empire, while Huáscar had the support of Cusco and the southern section. For five years, a civil war raged and countless Inca died.

In April 1532, while Atahualpa was busy setting up his own administrative center in the north, Huáscar was captured. Generals from Atahualpa's army killed many members of Huáscar's family and tied their bodies to poles along a highway leading out of Cusco. Atahualpa was sure his brother's capture would mean that he—Atahualpa—could finally ascend to the throne and take control of an empire he claimed was rightfully his.

But what neither brother knew was that a far greater outside threat was approaching. Led by an intrepid explorer named Francisco Pizarro, a small Spanish army was on its way down from Panama. For years, rumors had spread throughout

Europe about the vast wealth of the Inca Empire in the New World. Pizarro and his crew had gotten permission from Spain's King Charles I to claim the land and its resources and to establish a new Spanish province. They were ordered to conquer—or kill—the area's inhabitants in order to accomplish their mission.

The events that unfolded over the course of the following year were shocking to all involved. They were also gruesome and deadly. The Spanish conquest of the Inca Empire was one of the fastest and most systematic takedowns of an indigenous culture in history.

CHAPTER 2

SPANISH CONQUISTADORS INVADE

In the early 1530s, while Atahualpa and Huáscar were vying for power, the European conquest of Central and South America was already well underway. Just a few years earlier, Spanish explorer Hernán Cortés had led the successful takeover of Cuba. In 1519, he set his sights on claiming Mexico for the Spanish Crown. Over the next three years, his brutal exploits decimated much of the indigenous Aztec culture.

Francisco Pizarro, Cortés's contemporary, also hoped to secure territory and wealth for his country—and fame for himself. In 1513, he accompanied Spanish adventurer Vasco Núñez de Balboa on an exploratory trip to Panama to search for what he called the South Sea. During their journey, Balboa and Pizarro reached what is now known as the Pacific Ocean.

After the expedition ended, Pizarro's thirst for adventure didn't abate. In 1523, he organized two separate expeditions down the western coast of South America to scope out the landscape and determine the strength and vulnerability of its native people. Then in 1530, after receiving permission from the king, Pizarro picked a southern land he called Peru as his next target. (The name Peru was derived from a valley called Virú on the north coast.) He had heard about the Inca civil war and suspected that he could use the feud between Atahualpa and Huáscar to his advantage.

Spanish explorer and conquistador Francisco Pizarro lived from 1475 to 1541. He engineered the downfall of the Inca civilization.

Pizarro's plan was to send word to Atahualpa to request a meeting in the northern mountain town of Cajamarca. He proposed a lavish feast to celebrate the new Inca ruler's victory over his brother. What Atahualpa didn't realize was that Pizarro's plan involved a full-blown attack. Pizarro was a confident negotiator, but even he wasn't prepared for how easily the Inca would be subdued.

Joined by four of his brothers, Pizarro sailed for Panama in January 1530. By the following year, he was ready for the long

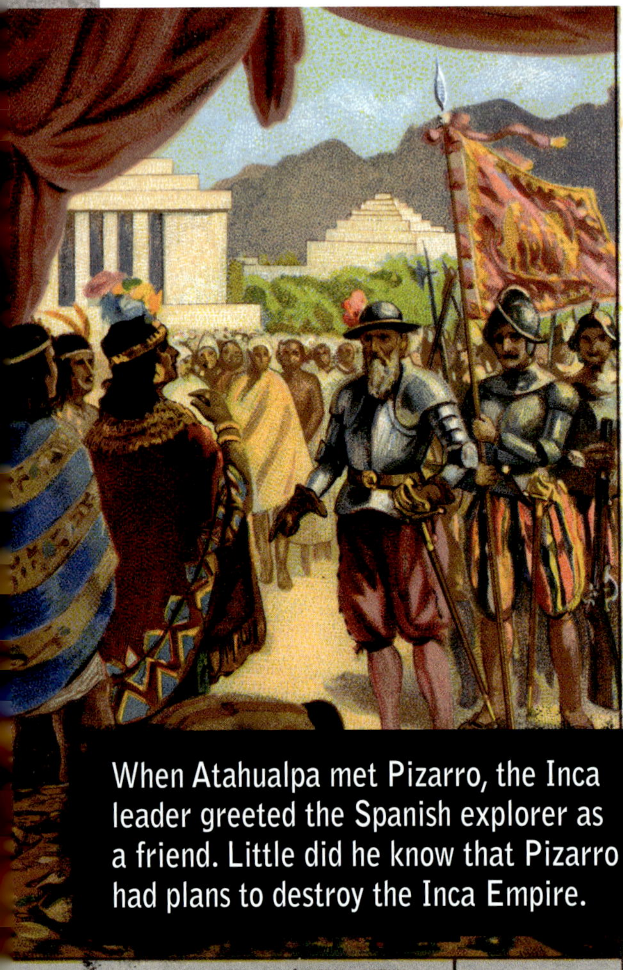

When Atahualpa met Pizarro, the Inca leader greeted the Spanish explorer as a friend. Little did he know that Pizarro had plans to destroy the Inca Empire.

journey south to Peru. He had just one ship, about 170 men in his entourage, and 37 horses on board.

A PLANNED AMBUSH AT CAJAMARCA

Pizarro and his small army arrived in Cajamarca on the eve of November 15, 1532. What they found was a scene unlike any they had ever seen before. A sea of tents covered the mountainside, stretching far into the horizon. Tens of thousands of Inca (estimates range from thirty thousand to more than eighty thousand) milled among the many campfires. The Spanish were clearly outnumbered.

The next morning Pizarro sent a message to Atahualpa. He requested that the Inca ruler meet him in Cajamarca's main plaza, giving his assurance that no harm would come to him. In fact, Pizarro planned to ambush him.

To prepare for the ambush, Pizarro ordered his soldiers

to line the outskirts of the square. He divided the cavalry and infantry into two groups on either side. Then he sent a few men with muskets, small artillery, and trumpets up to the small fort above the plaza. He told each of his men that when he gave the signal, they should blare the trumpets and attack. The Inca, of course, knew nothing about the trap they were about to fall into.

As the Inca began to arrive, the Spanish were once again amazed by what they saw. First came a wave of Inca warriors, dressed in vibrant colors. Then came three waves of dancers and singers, twirling and chanting traditional Inca songs. Finally, Atahualpa arrived on a litter (a type of chair hoisted high in the air) with a cushion that was covered in gold, silver, and parrot

INCA RICHES

Aside from an interest in land and converting the South American "heathens" to the Christian faith, one of the conquistadors' main reasons for conquering the Inca was to steal their precious metals. The Inca had been crafting magnificent artifacts out of gold, silver, and copper since the 1400s. They made elegant gold necklaces, earrings, and ornaments to wear in their noses. Goblets made out of pounded platinum were commonplace, as were copper ceremonial vessels. Because flaunting one's riches was seen as a sign of power, members of the Inca elite were often buried alongside their treasures, with piles upon piles of exquisite objects filling up their tombs.

feathers and draped in luscious fabric. He wore a gold crown on his head and a necklace full of gleaming emeralds. Behind him, two smaller litters carried Inca high chiefs and a squadron of Inca warriors wearing gold crowns filled out the procession.

THE SPANISH ATTACK

When Atahualpa reached the center of the plaza, Pizarro sent a priest, Friar Vicente de Valverde, to speak to him. With a cross in one hand and a Bible in the other, Friar de Valverde approached the Inca ruler. Atahualpa asked for the book, even though he and the rest of the Inca were illiterate. When he had the Bible in hand, he threw it down on the ground in disgust. Furious, the friar announced to the Spanish that the Inca were enemies of Christianity.

With that, Pizarro gave the signal his army was waiting for. Trumpets sounded and the Spanish soldiers poured out of their hiding spots, attacking the Inca with brutal force. They used guns, steel swords, daggers, and spears—weapons the Inca had never seen before—to slice through their enemies as quickly and thoroughly as possible. To add to the chaos, Pizarro and his men had tied rattles around the horses' legs. The noise of the pounding hooves and the rattles terrified the Inca even more.

One by one, the Inca were ruthlessly cut down by the Spanish. Because the Inca hadn't expected a battle, most of them were unarmed and had no way of protecting themselves against the slaughter. Instead, they were so caught by surprise and so full of fear that those who weren't murdered

More than seven thousand Inca warriors were killed trying to protect their leader from the Spanish. This nineteenth-century painting of the incident is by the British artist John Everett Millais.

got trampled to death in their desperate attempts to escape.

Amid the mayhem, Pizarro boldly entered the fray and headed straight toward Atahualpa's litter. At that moment, the emperor was still safe, held aloft by a series of loyal warriors who, when stabbed, were immediately replaced by reinforcements. But not for long. The Spanish cavalry rode in and, using their spears, toppled the litter to its side. Atahualpa rolled out and was captured. In a mere two hours, more than

HOW WERE THE INCA DEFEATED SO QUICKLY?

When studying the destruction of the Inca civilization, perhaps the most baffling mystery to solve is how a massive army could be defeated by fewer than two hundred men. The answer is tragic, but simple: the Spanish had the upper hand. They knew the Andean natives didn't have sophisticated weapons like spears and guns. They also knew they'd be the only soldiers on horses, which were unfamiliar animals to the Inca, and thus could attack from above. Add the cacophony of noise, the element of surprise, and the fact that the Spanish army's attack methods didn't conform to the Andean codes of ritualized warfare, and the Inca didn't have a chance. There were too many of them in the square; those who tried to escape got trampled. By the time they could even think to send for reinforcements with weapons (only wooden clubs, rudimentary axes, and slingshots, which could maim but not kill), Pizarro and his men had already captured Atahualpa and fled to safety. None of the Spanish soldiers died in the fight.

seven thousand Inca were killed, with many more wounded.

ATAHUALPA'S CAPTURE

Aside from Atahualpa, all the lords and high chiefs in the newly established Inca government were fatally stabbed, shot, or beheaded during the battle. As for Atahualpa, he was taken hostage by the Spanish and sentenced to burn at the stake. Pizarro's secretary, Francisco de Xeres, reported that the Spanish commander told Atahualpa:

> *Do not take it as an insult that you have been defeated and taken prisoner … We come to conquer this land by [the King of Spain's] command, that all may come to a knowledge of God and of His Holy Catholic Faith; and by reason of our good mission, God, the Creator of heaven and earth and of all things in them, permits this, in order that you may know Him and come out from the bestial and diabolical life that you lead.*

Atahualpa had been beaten. But the larger battle wasn't over—at least not yet. He bribed Pizarro to get out of his sentence. Knowing the Spanish's appetite for gold, he offered to fill a large room "once with gold and twice with silver" within two months' time.

The Spanish took the bait. They agreed to imprison Atahualpa in Cajamarca's Sun Temple in exchange for the ransom. In the meantime, Pizarro schemed new ways to use Atahualpa's influence over his kingdom against him. Little did the once-omnipotent Inca emperor know that he was about to fall into another deadly trap.

CHAPTER 3

PLUNDER AND OPPRESSION

By the end of 1532, Francisco Pizarro had sent word to Spain that his mission to topple the Inca emperor from his throne was complete. Now came the second half of the operation—to assume control over Atahualpa's kingdom by subduing the Inca people through whatever means necessary. His first step was to figure out not only how to get rich off of his subjects, but also how to underhandedly gain their trust while doing so.

In 1533, Atahualpa was still imprisoned in Cajamarca's Sun Temple. Per his agreement with Pizarro, he made arrangements for large quantities of gold and silver to be brought to the Spanish invaders in exchange for his release. Though his true intentions cannot be known, many historians believe that Atahualpa hoped this gift would inspire the Spanish to treat the Inca leader as both captive and honored guest—just like the Incas had done in the past with the leaders of ethnic groups they defeated during battle.

During his life, Atahualpa accumulated a large fortune of gold and jewels. Most of it was stolen by Pizarro and the Spanish invaders.

This was not the case. While Atahualpa was interned, Pizarro called for Spanish reinforcements. He also sent a team down to Cusco to acquire even more gold and precious metals for the Spanish Crown. The Spaniards plundered the city without mercy, showing no regard for the sanctity of Inca relics. They stole valuable vases, goblets, and jewelry. They also ripped off large segments of a gold-plated wall inside Qorikancha, the Inca Empire's holiest temple dedicated to Inti the Sun God.

Once his men had a good portion of the treasures in hand, Pizarro ordered them to melt the objects into bricks of gold and silver. A fifth of the proceeds were sent back to Spain. The rest, he distributed among his team.

He then made a decision about Atahualpa's fate. There had been disagreement about what to do with the Inca leader. Some members of Pizarro's army believed Atahualpa would be

Atahualpa was executed by the Spanish in the summer of 1533. This painting of the Inca leader's funeral was painted by the Peruvian artist Luis Montero in 1876.

most useful as a puppet ruler—the Spanish could force him to do their bidding or suffer the consequences. Others believed Atahualpa was too powerful even in prison and posed too much of a threat; his loyalists could plan a rescue that would inevitably impede the Spaniards' mission.

Ultimately Pizarro decided against sparing the Inca leader. On July 26, 1533, Atahualpa was escorted into the Cajamarca plaza and tied to a stake. Because the Inca believed that the soul could not go on to the afterlife if the physical body was burned, Atahualpa reluctantly agreed to be baptized as Christian. Then, he was put to death by strangulation. Some historians believe that some of Atahualpa's followers later exhumed his body, mummified it, and secretly buried it somewhere in the north of his empire amidst a pile of golden treasure. His body has never been found.

ONWARD TO CUSCO

Fresh on the heels of Atahualpa's death, Pizarro and his men began the long journey south to Cusco in order to take over the Inca capital and establish their control over the region. As with their original conquest, their army was small. With fewer than 100 men on horseback and some on foot, they faced an uphill battle.

Along the way, the Spanish encountered much resistance from the Inca people. Those still loyal to Atahualpa, who hoped to avenge his death, did everything they could to hinder Spanish progression. They built barriers in the roads and raided storehouses of all supplies. They burned down rope suspension bridges, forcing Pizarro and his men to descend perilous cliffs and ford gushing rivers, such as the Apurimac, to reach the other side. And they waged confrontations in areas such as Hatun Xauxa and Vilcashuamán, with casualties on both sides.

But leftover factions of Huáscar loyalists (Atahualpa's rivals) provided the Spaniards with information and aided them in battle. With their help, the conquistadors were ultimately victorious. On November 15, 1533, they arrived in Cusco unimpeded and set up shop. Once again, Pizarro knew how to exploit the Inca people. He installed Manco Capac as a co-ruler of the empire. Manco was another of Atahualpa's brothers, and he had the support of Huáscar's followers and the Cusco elite.

For the Inca people, the relief at seeing one of their own in charge despite the foreigners' intrusion was short-lived. They soon realized that Manco had no real power of his own. Instead, he was forced to do the Spaniards' bidding, even if it meant taking away the rights of his people. The conquistadors also continued to loot everything of value from Cusco's buildings and homes, including what was left in the great temple of Qorikancha.

As Manco witnessed the oppression of his people, he increasingly understood that he could not continue to exist as a lackey for Pizarro and his men. Instead, he pledged to become a leader for the resistance against the European intruders. After a failed attempt to flee Cusco in late 1535, Manco escaped the following year. He began recruiting soldiers for an army. It became Manco's goal to fight the conquistadors and win—or die trying.

FAILED RESISTANCE

In early May 1536, Manco staged an attack on Pizarro's Cusco. The Inca resistance had amassed somewhere between 200,000 and 400,000 troops, who descended on the imperial city en masse. They used slingshots to hurl hot stones wrapped in cotton to set the city's thatched roofs ablaze. They flooded the plains surrounding the city to prevent the Spaniards from accessing

From 1535 to 1541, Lima grew into a cosmopolitan city. After 1542, it became not only the capital of Peru, but a cultural center for much of South America.

supplies or reinforcements. And they used Sacsahuamán as a military stronghold to rain down attacks from above.

But despite their cunning and persistence, the Inca were still no match for the Spanish and their weapons. By the end of the month, the Spaniards had regained control of Cusco. Manco and his troops withdrew.

While the attack on Cusco was taking place, another battle was being waged on the coast in a new city called Lima. Just as they did in Cusco, Inca resistance fighters stormed into the city,

THE BIRTH OF LIMA

On January 18, 1535, the city of Lima—Peru's modern-day capital—was founded by Francisco Pizarro. Called the Ciudad de los Reyes ("City of the Kings"), Lima replaced Cusco as the new center of commerce because of its close proximity to the coast. As the region's port, it could import and export supplies, receive communications from Spain, and welcome hoards of new Europeans eager to explore a new continent. It also became the seat of government. In 1542, Spain designated Lima the capital of the Viceroyalty of Peru. The high courts also relocated to Lima, allowing the Spanish to rule with impunity over vast portions of South America. Lima became an important religious center, too. A Roman Catholic diocese was established in the city in 1541.

outnumbering the Spanish. But once again the conquistadors had the upper hand. When the Inca warriors arrived with their commanding officers at the head, the Spaniards attacked them from both sides with guns and spears, killing them instantly. What was left of the distraught Inca army fled into the surrounding hillsides.

Manco initiated another uprising in 1538. The revolt spread from the central Peruvian highlands down to Lake Titicaca and the Charcas region in the south. Though this rebellion also failed, his persistent efforts sparked a nationalist movement throughout the shaky Inca Empire. Manco and his

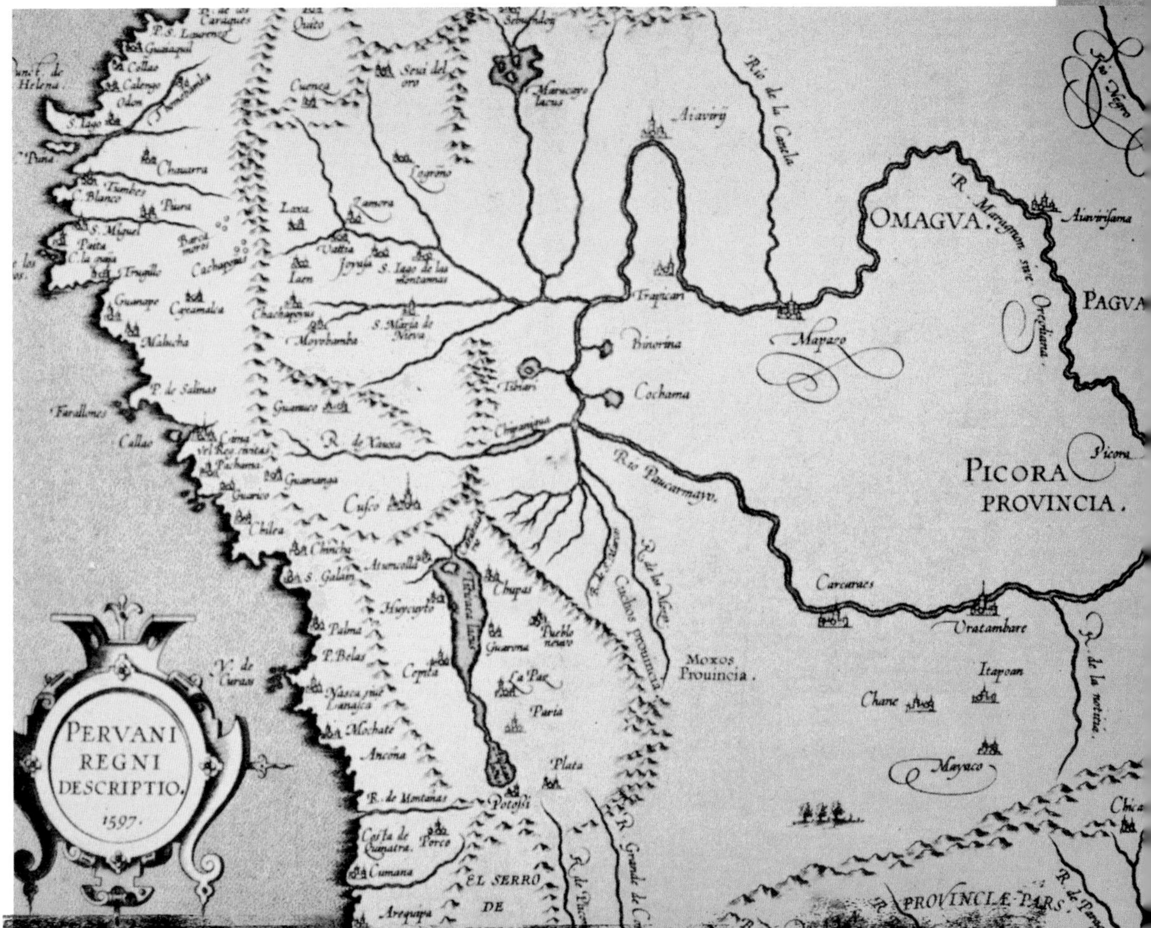

This map is of the Viceroyalty of Peru. Created in 1542, the Viceroyalty of Peru was a colonial administrative unit that included all of the parts of South America that were under Spanish control.

followers regrouped to a region called the Vilcabamba province. For years, they initiated mini surprise-attacks on unsuspecting Spanish caravans traveling the road between Cusco and Lima. The Inca guerrillas stole supplies and staged small acts of sabotage. The Spaniards tried to coax Manco back to Cusco and become a puppet ruler once again. But Manco refused. Ultimately, he was murdered by a group of Spaniards in 1544. The resistance movement he started continued in his absence.

Unfortunately, the thrill of tiny victories felt by the rebels did not trickle down to the majority of the Inca people. As more and more Spanish flocked to and settled in Lima, Cusco, and the surrounding region, an increasing number of the Incas' rights were stripped away. Over the next three decades, life under colonial rule grew more and more oppressive. The systematic and fully intentional destruction of the Inca Empire was well underway.

CHAPTER 4

THE DEMISE OF THE INCA CIVILIZATION

The Inca resistance led by Manco's successors maintained an independent state in the Vilcabamba province for the next thirty-six years. One leader—Titu Cusi—even drafted a lengthy letter to the Spanish crown, asking for a peaceful co-existence as rulers of two independent regions. But while Titu and other more aggressive resistance fighters were busy scheming ways to take back Cusco and Lima, life in those cities was getting progressively worse for the indigenous people.

Over the next four decades, the Spaniards acted on their plan to methodically subjugate the Inca people and erase whatever traces of traditions and culture they had left. Their methods were simple: crush the Inca's strength by mandating resettlement and initiating a ruthless system of forced labor; abuse the Inca women by coercing them into unequal marriages or sexual slavery; and obliterate the Inca's hope and identity by disallowing the practice of sacred rituals and enforcing religious conversion to Christianity.

ENSLAVED LABOR PRACTICES

As colonialism began to take root throughout Peru and the surrounding areas, and as the Spanish commandeered more and more control of the disintegrating Inca Empire, a number of troubling changes took place. First, so that the new rulers could keep watch over their subjects, tens of thousands of native people were forcefully resettled out of their communities and into new towns near commercial centers. Here they could be supervised for signs of rebellion. Consequently, much of the painstakingly cared-for countryside was reluctantly abandoned and the terraced gardens full of crops deteriorated into ruin.

In colonial Peru, the indigenous people were considered lower class. Some were kept as slaves. This image illustrating the cruelty of the Spanish is by the sixteenth-century engraver and editor Theodor de Bry.

After the forced resettlement, the Spanish Crown now had an easily exploitable and expendable indigenous population in or near the cities. They introduced the ethnicity-based *encomienda* system and used the Inca *mita*—mandatory public service—as a way of ratcheting up the workforce. Each conquistador was granted one or more Inca natives as his personal workers. Though still illiterate, they were taught to speak Spanish and were required to work long hours for very little to no allowance, usually under extremely harsh conditions.

In the burgeoning city of Lima, for example, this type of slave labor was responsible for replacing most of the adobe-style buildings that were common at the time with newer Colonial-style architecture. Lima's plazas—beloved meeting places for the Inca—were removed to make way for gridded streets. Outside the city, enormous haciendas were constructed, allowing the Spanish plantation owners to live in luxury. The native population, on the other hand, worked the land like dogs and grew crops that were foreign to their diet, such as rice, sugar, and wheat. Over time, a bourgeois Spanish elite emerged that controlled the land and ran the economy, while indigenous Peruvians remained uneducated and powerless.

Perhaps the most egregious form of Spanish exploitation took place in the mines. After the Spaniards looted every nook and cranny in the cities for Inca gold and silver, they searched the surrounding countryside for "undiscovered" natural resources. What they uncovered was a goldmine—literally. Throughout the latter half of the sixteenth century, the Spanish Crown made the modern equivalent of trillions of dollars off of

This illustration shows Cerro Rico and Potosí, the city at the foot of the mountain. Cerro Rico contains the Potosí silver mine, which was a source of wealth for the Spanish but a place of misery for native workers.

the minerals mined in northern Peru and what is now Bolivia. And as with the encomienda system in the cities, the Spaniards did none of the actual work.

One member of each indigenous family was required to work underground, mining gold or silver. The conditions were dark, dusty, and extraordinarily brutal. When one family member died on the job, which usually happened within a year or two, the family was obliged to send in a substitute.

THE LEGEND OF CERRO RICO: POTOSÍ SILVER MINE

At its peak, Potosí Silver Mine was the largest depository of silver in the world. Often referred to as Cerro Rico—or "rich hill"—it was discovered almost by accident. In 1545, a native Peruvian named Diego Huallpa was working at the Porco mine. There were rumors of an old Inca shrine located at the top of a neighboring 15,800-foot (4,816-m) mountain, and his Spanish overseer ordered him to climb up and investigate it. On his way down, a gust of wind caused Huallpa to trip, and he dug his hand into the red dirt for traction. When he lifted up his fist, it was filled with silver ore.

The conquistadors rushed to stake a claim on Potosí's riches and made a fortune for the Spanish Crown. Today, Potosí Silver Mine is still in commission—and just as deadly as ever. Locals call it "the Mountain that Eats Men" because of the scores of men and boys who die there every year. There aren't any gas detectors, and only the drillers are allowed to wear masks. Some miners die by falling down seemingly bottomless well shafts. But most succumb to silicosis, a lethal lung disease that is caused by breathing in rock particles.

According to Felipe Calizaya, a Bolivian professor of mining engineering at the University of Utah, there is little doubt that the Potosí Silver Mine is one of the most dangerous places in the world to work as a miner.

Under such circumstances, thousands of Inca perished. The increasingly wealthy Spanish didn't bat an eye at the death toll.

ENFORCED CONCUBINAGE AND RELIGIOUS CONVERSION

There's no question that the Spanish took advantage of Inca men by enforcing a cruel and incapacitating work load. But some might argue that circumstances were worse for the Inca women. Many were taken as concubines—women who live with a man but either have a lower status than his wife or are ordered to become sexual partners against their will. Some of these women got pregnant and had illegitimate children who weren't entitled to their father's wealth. Others were forced into relationships with men a half-century older. In fact, one of Francisco Pizarro's concubines was only fifteen years old at the time that their relationship started, while he was sixty-five.

But perhaps the most devastating result of Spanish imperialism was the deliberate annihilation of Inca cultural traditions and spiritual practices. Throughout their reign, the conquistadors forbade the Inca from practicing most of their holy rituals, believing the customs to be blasphemous and akin to devil worship. For example, in Cusco in 1558, the Spanish discovered that descendants of Inca kings were worshiping the mummies of their dead ancestors and offering sacrifices in their honor, as was common practice in the Inca religion. The Spanish removed the mummies and transported them to the coast, and destroyed the icons of the rulers.

The Church and Convent of Santo Domingo was built on the ruins of Qorikancha, one of the most revered temples in all of Peru.

The Spanish also tried to forcefully convert as many indigenous people to Christianity as possible, using Quechua—the dominant language of the Andean people—to teach them the basics of their new required religion. They tore down sacred Inca temples and replaced them with Catholic churches that became the centerpiece of every village or major city's central plaza. They sent indigenous children to Christian-based schools run by Catholic missionaries. Many of the classes involved Bible

WAS IT GENOCIDE?

The word "genocide" was coined in the twentieth century to refer to the deliberate, organized attempts to wipe out whole ethnic groups during the Holocaust in the 1940s and the Armenian genocide in the 1910s and 1920s. Some people hesitate to use the term "genocide" to refer to the atrocities of earlier eras. Others carefully restrict its use to incidents in which the primary aim of the perpetrators is to annihilate a people. They argue that the destruction of Inca lives and traditions was the brutal means to an end (expanding Spanish wealth and power), rather then the goal in and of itself. Also, while the native peoples of Peru suffered unfair treatment both under colonialism and after it ended, indigenous elements remain ingrained in Peruvian culture today. It's much easier to see the traces of Inca civilization in Peru than it is to recognize the Native American cultures that existed in most parts of the United States, for example.

The mass murder and subjugation of the Inca differs from similar horrific events that have taken place throughout the twentieth century. But huge numbers of native peoples were mercilessly killed. The ongoing, deliberate attempts to break the identity of the Inca people and stamp out Inca ways of life are best understood as cultural genocide.

study and all children were required to look and dress as Euro-centric as possible. Traditional songs and dances were outlawed. All churchgoers were required to go to confession.

The majority of the Inca abhorred this turn of events, though they begrudgingly followed orders. But one small underground faction tried to rebel and enacted the Taki Onqoy, or "Dancing Sickness" movement. They shunned European rules whenever possible and practiced a ritual wherein dancers worked themselves up into frenzied trances to worship traditional Andean gods. Some historians believe these spiritual rebels amassed a small amount of weapons in hopes of staging an armed rebellion against the Spanish. The movement was squashed, however, when one of its participants revealed the movement's plans during a forced Catholic confession. Many of the Taki Onqoy members were killed.

THE INCA EMPIRE CRUMBLES

By the 1570s, the Spanish conquistadors had cemented themselves as the new leaders of the Andean region. Francisco Pizarro was long dead—he had been murdered by a fellow rival in 1541. But his successors picked up where he left off, oppressing the indigenous population with full approval from the royal court in Spain.

As for the last vestiges of Inca rebel forces: they, too, met a gruesome end. After Manco died in 1544, he was replaced by his son, Sayri Túpac, then by Titu Cusi, and finally by Túpac Amaru. In June 1572, a faction of Spanish soldiers advanced on the rebel sanctuary of Vilcabamba. They captured the Inca leader, marched him into the central plaza, forced a conversion to Catholicism, and cut off his head.

Túpac Amaru was the last leader of the Inca. He was executed by the Spanish in 1572. This portrait of him is by an unknown eighteenth-century artist.

Túpac's violent death signaled the end of Inca resistance to Spanish imperialism. With the fall of Vilcabama, the short reign of one of the most powerful empires in history came to its conclusion. By that time, the Andean population had dwindled to nearly eighty percent of what it once was. In some coastal areas the numbers plummeted to as little as one-twentieth of its size in 1532. In less than fifty years the mighty Inca civilization had crumbled.

CHAPTER 5

INCA TRADITIONS LIVE ON

In 1572, the Inca Empire officially came to an end. Because of a variety of factors—malnutrition, exposure to European diseases, ongoing civil strife, and compulsory labor practices—the population of the indigenous people had dwindled to an estimated 2.7 million, a tiny fraction of what it once was. The Spanish had succeeded in colonizing the region. Over the next three hundred years, they continued to exert their control over all aspects of Andean society, including urban development, government policies and infrastructure, religious practices, and cultural expression.

On July 28, 1821, Peru finally won back its independence. But the end of Spanish rule didn't provide many solutions to the myriad political, social, and economic problems facing the country (a heavily imbalanced class system being just one example). In fact, the transition from being a dependent colony

Though it was built during the twentieth century, Lima's City Hall is in the Spanish Colonial style. The building is officially known as the Municipal Palace of Lima.

to a liberated nation proved to be much more difficult than the Peruvians had anticipated.

Even today, the influence of colonial Spain can be felt throughout the country. Spanish is the dominant language in Peru and in much of South America; it is spoken by approximately 84 percent of Peruvians. It is also the official language of the Peruvian government, the media, and the country's education system. The rest of the population speaks Quechua (13 percent) and a mix of other native languages.

Because of the Spanish conquistadors' aggressive conversion tactics in the sixteenth century, Catholicism is still Peru's main religion. Today, 81 percent of Peruvians are Roman Catholic. Evangelicals make up 12 percent of the population. The rest, especially those who live in rural areas, adhere to their traditional faiths.

The class divide between the elite and the peasants still exists as well. This is a direct result of the land-ownership and labor practices initiated during the colonial years. Today, Quechua Indians constitute almost half of Peru's population. Mestizos—people of mixed Indian and European heritage—make up nearly one-third. People of European descent make

THE SHINING PATH

In the 1980s and 1990s, Peru went through a tumultuous period. A guerrilla rebel group called the Shining Path terrorized the region and inflicted waves of violence upon the Peruvian people. Led by Abimael Guzmán, its members adopted the teachings of China's communist leader Mao Zedong. They modeled their revolutionary movement after China's Cultural Revolution and recruited scores of indigenous people to fight in their army. Historians estimate that between sixty thousand and eighty thousand people died. Nearly 75 percent of those murdered were indigenous Quechua speakers, who made up less than 20 percent of the population at the time.

up just one-eighth of the population, yet they are the ones who control much of the country's wealth. A large portion of the land claimed by the wealthy conquistadors still remains in the hands of the upper class. Bustling urban centers like Lima and Arequipa continue to be the most intellectually and culturally modern sections of the country. The people in these areas tend to be educated, with managerial or professional jobs. The more rural areas, where many indigenous people still live, often lack sufficient resources and receive little to no help from the government.

Though technically a modern term, many historians suggest that what happened to the Inca civilization and its people can retroactively be categorized as cultural and ideological genocide. The effects of this genocide can still be felt today. Despite this pervasive problem, much is being done to revive—and even revere—the Inca culture. Many of the old problems still exist. But over the last few centuries, the Inca civilization has begun to experience a sort of slow renaissance.

APPRECIATION OF INCA TRADITIONS

When visiting Peru, it's hard not to notice Spain's influence, especially in the cities. Much of the architecture is from the colonial period and there is a cathedral—usually Catholic—around every corner. Upon further inspection, however, it's clear that Inca cultural traditions are making their way back into the public consciousness after centuries of suppression. What's more, some of these traditions never completely vanished.

In Cusco, for example, Quechua women still sit in one of the city's many plazas, weaving traditional rugs and garments on backstrap looms. Sprawling outdoor markets featuring vegetables, meat, and goods trucked in from the highlands and other rural farming areas (usually held on Wednesday or during the weekend) remain an integral part of both urban and rural life. Museums such as the Museo Nacional de Arqueología, Antropología e Historia del Perú in Lima, and the Museo de Arte Religioso del Perú in Cusco showcase both archaeological relics from the pre-Columbian period and modern artistic treasures created by contemporary painters, potters, and weavers.

Today, Peruvian women still sell their woven goods in many of the public squares throughout Cusco.

Despite the dominance of Catholicism and Spanish efforts to quash any dissenters, a number of the Inca's religious traditions and celebrations are still practiced throughout Peru today. In the highlands, offerings of coca and *chica*, a fermented drink usually derived from corn maize, are still made to Pachamama, the Earth Mother. These offerings are made to give thanks for a successful harvest. Qoyllur Rit'i, a festival celebrating the reappearance of the Pleiades constellation, and Inti Raymi, a pilgrimage to honor the Inti (one of the most worshiped gods in the Inca religion), are celebrated in Cusco every year. Peruvians embark on a trek to high-elevation shrines, offering up food and gifts to mini totems along the way. These festivals are a way to commune with family and keep old traditions alive.

There is also Peru's recent influx of tourism. In 2016, the number of tourists increased to nearly 4.6 billion, up from 2.2 billion the year before. (The all-time low was less than 217,000 in 1992.) Visitors can enjoy an eight-day trek through the Sacred Valley and climb up to the "lost city" of Machu Picchu. They can hike more than half a mile down to the bottom of Colca Canyon—the world's deepest river canyon and a habitat for the giant Andean condor. Or they can arrange a wide variety of agro-tourism packages that might include stays with indigenous host families, tours of artist cooperatives, and cooking lessons to learn how to make ancient Inca dishes.

The increase in tourism has its own set of problems—erosion, pollution, and a strain on the country's resources, to name a few. But the uptick in interest from afar affords new opportunities to

Tourism continues to flourish in Peru. Here, a black-chested buzzard eagle lands on a tourist's arm in Maca, a small village in Peru's Colca Canyon.

showcase and appreciate Peruvian culture and traditions, both modern and ancient.

A CHANGING PERSPECTIVE

The Inca civilization fell more than four hundred years ago. In the past century, Peru has slowly made a bit of progress. The country has suffered through a few transitional governments

HOW YOU CAN FIGHT HATE

In very simple terms, the Inca civilization was destroyed because one group thought they were better than another. Sadly, there are many other examples of this throughout history and today, including the Yazidi Genocide in modern-day Iraq and the ethnic cleansing taking place in Syria. But there are many actions you can take to combat hatred, racism, and other acts of violence.

Read as much as you can about what's going on. If the problem is happening in another country, read the newspaper and reputable online news sources every day to keep updated on the situation's progress.

Write letters to members of your legislature, if the problem is happening closer to home. Better yet, call your representatives and explain why you're against the atrocities taking place. Ask if there's something you can do to help or how you can get involved in your community.

Listen to the stories of people who are being attacked or discriminated against. Learn about their opinions and perspective on topics of race, ethnicity, gender, and others in order to understand what they're going through.

Volunteer for organizations that support positive change and the acceptance of all people and beliefs. Amnesty International, Human Rights Watch, the Peace Corps, and Youth for Human Rights International are just a few nonprofit organizations working to promote the greater good throughout the world.

Check your privilege. You may have had the fortunate experience of growing up without having to face oppression, abuse, or prejudice. But that's not the reality for a majority of people. Practice simple acts of kindness every day. Go out of your way to help those in need. Think better; be better. If you see something, say something.

since its independence, including a number of brutal military coups and corrupt dictatorships. But in 1993, it adopted a new constitution that called for a popularly elected president, who serves as chief of state and head of the government for a five-year term. Voting is now mandatory for all citizens ages eighteen to seventy and, as of 2003, women must constitute at least 30 percent of all candidates on political party lists.

Indigenous Peruvians are still mostly poor and marginalized. But they are also speaking out more than ever. In 2001, the country's first president of indigenous ancestry, Alejandro Toledo, was democratically elected and served until 2006. Human rights activist Hilaria Supa was elected to the Peruvian Congress in 2006. She took her oath in Quechua, becoming the first parliamentarian in Peru's history to do so in any indigenous language.

In mid-December 2016, a national news program called *Ñuqanchik*—which means "all of us"—aired entirely in Quechua for the first time in Peru's history. For co-presenter Marisol Mena the broadcast was a groundbreaking achievement. "We've

Hilaria Supa is a revered defender of abused minorities, including her own people.

struggled for a long time to see this initiative and now we are broadcasting information to our Quechua brothers and sisters," she said.

Prime Minister Fernando Zevala agreed. "This, we believe, will transform the relationship between the government, the state, and those people who speak a language different from Spanish," he said.

In today's accelerated world, the way we choose to live is changing. Societies are becoming increasingly modern and technology-dependent. Ancient traditions are discarded to make way for new ways of thinking. But the Inca legacy lives on. In the face of change, there is clearly room for everyone.

TIMELINE

1100 Inca tribes first appear in South America, near what is modern-day Peru.

1438 Cusi Inca Yupanqui (Pachacuti) becomes the ninth emperor of the Inca Empire. He reorganizes his kingdom into the Tawantinsuyu, with Cusco as the capital.

1493 Pachacuti's son, Túpac Inca, dies; his territory stretches into modern-day Colombia and Ecuador.

1513 Vasco Núñez de Balboa and Francisco Pizarro reach the Pacific Ocean.

1521 The Aztec capital of Tenochtitlán falls to the conquistador Hernán Cortés.

1527 Huayna Capac and his heir, Ninan Cuyuchi, die, setting off a civil war and rivalry for control between half-brothers Atahualpa and Huáscar.

1532 On November 16, Spanish conquistador Francisco Pizarro and his small army invade Peru, attacking Atahualpa's army at Cajamarca. The Spanish are victorious.

1533 Atahualpa is executed by the Spanish on July 26. On November 15, the Spanish enter Cusco and install Manco Capac as a puppet leader.

1535 Lima is founded on January 18. Manco tries to flee Cusco in late fall.

1536 Manco stages an attack on the Spanish invaders in May; it fails.

1538 Manco initiates a second uprising against the Spanish; it fails again. He and the rebel army resettle in Vilcabamba.

1541 Francisco Pizarro is murdered by a rival.

1542 Spain officially designates Lima as capital of the Viceroyalty of Peru.

1544 Manco dies.

1545 Diego Huallpa discovers Cerro Ricco, which quickly becomes the Potosí Silver Mine.

1558 The Spanish discover the Inca practice of worshiping their former rulers' mummies and banish the practice.

1572 The Spanish invade the last Inca stronghold in Vilcabamba and behead their leader, Túpac Amaru. Vilcabamba falls, signaling the official end of the Inca civilization.

1821 Peru wins its independence from Spain on July 28.

1911 The American explorer Hiram Bingham III rediscovers Machu Picchu.

1941 The word "genocide" is coined by lawyer Raphael Lemkin.

2001 Alejandro Toledo, Peru's first president of indigenous ancestry, is elected.

2006 Hilaria Supa becomes the first parliamentarian in Peru's history to take the oath in any indigenous language.

2016 A news program airs in Quechua for the first time in Peru's history; it's called *Ñuqanchik*.

GLOSSARY

annihilate To completely destroy.

blasphemous Against God; irreligious or profane.

bourgeois Characteristic of the middle or upper class; materialistic.

burgeoning Blooming; developing; thriving.

cavalry Soldiers who fought on horseback.

colonialism The practice of acquiring control over another country by occupying it with settlers, taking hold of its political processes, and exploiting it socially and economically.

conquistadors Conquerors, usually referring to the Spanish resettlement of Peru during the sixteenth century.

conversion In religious terms, when a person undergoes a transformation from one religion to another and agrees to accept the main tenets of the new religion.

coup Violent and illegal takeover of power from a government.

decimate To destroy or wipe out almost completely.

depose To forcefully remove from office.

diocese An area that is under the control of a bishop in the Christian church.

diversity The presence of different types of people from a variety of cultures or racial backgrounds in a group or organization.

egregious Shocking; very bad.

ethnic Relating to a population subgroup that has a common national or racial makeup or cultural tradition.

genocide The methodical and deliberate destruction of a racial, political, or cultural group.

guerrilla A fighter who is part of a small, independent force, not the regular armed forces.

hacienda A huge mansion or plantation, usually in Spanish-speaking regions.

illiterate Unable to read or write.

impunity Free from punishment or consequences.

indigenous Native to a certain place or country.

intrepid Bold; adventurous.

nomadic Moving from place to place; wandering.

omnipotent All-powerful.

pervasive All-encompassing.

prolific Plentiful; fertile.

prospector An explorer who specifically searches for rich land.

relic A fragment of something, particularly something with a deep, often religious, meaning.

revere Respect; admire.

rudimentary Very simple and basic.

subjugation Bringing someone or something under one's complete control.

FOR MORE INFORMATION

American Museum of Natural History
1200 New York Avenue NW
Washington, DC 20005
(202) 326-6400
Website: http://www.aaas.org
Facebook: @naturalhistory
Twitter: @AMNH
Inside this vast museum, the Hall of South American Peoples features the art, tools, technologies, and traditions of the continent's pre-Columbian cultures, including the Inca.

Field Museum
1400 South Lake Shore Drive
Chicago, IL 60605
(312) 922-9410
Website: https://www.fieldmuseum.org
Facebook: @fieldmuseum
Twitter: @FieldMuseum
Visitors to the Field Museum can view ceramics from the Inca civilization, whose conflicts with the Spanish was among the most dramatic and far-reaching in ancient history.

Metropolitan Museum of Art
1000 Fifth Avenue
New York, NY 10028
(212) 662-3397
Website: http://www.metmuseum.org
Facebook: @metmuseum
Twitter: @metmuseum

This museum's collection from the ancient Americas spans more than three thousand years. Examples of Inca garments and tapestries, silver, and pottery are on display.

Museum of Anthropology at the University of British Columbia
6393 NW Marine Drive
Vancouver, BC V6T 1Z2
Canada
(604) 827-5932
Website: http://moa.ubc.ca
Facebook: @MOAUBC
Twitter: @MOA_UBC
The museum houses extensive First Nation–centric collections from around the world, including more than four thousand original objects and textiles from Central and South America.

Peabody Museum of Archaeology and Ethnology
Harvard University
11 Divinity Avenue
Cambridge, MA 02138
(617) 496-1027
Website: https://www.peabody.harvard.edu
Visitors can find more than five thousand ancient Peruvian textiles on display, as well as Inca pottery, metalwork, and even an example of a quipu.

WEBSITES

Because of the changing nature of internet links, Rosen Publishing has developed an online list of websites related to the subject of this book. Use this link to access the list:

http://www.rosenlinks.com/BWGE/Inca

FOR FURTHER READING

Aztec, Inca & Maya (DK Eyewitness Books). New York, NY: DK Children, 2011.

Gruber, Beth. *National Geographic Investigates Ancient Inca*. Washington, DC: National Geographic, 2007.

Machajewski, Sarah. *The Ancient Inca Economy* (Spotlight on the Maya, Aztec, and Inca Civilizations). New York, NY: Rosen Publishing, 2017.

Morlock, Theresa. *Ancient Inca Geography* (Spotlight on the Maya, Aztec, and Inca Civilizations). New York, NY: Rosen Publishing, 2017.

Nagelhout, Ryan. *Ancient Inca Technology* (Spotlight on the Maya, Aztec, and Inca Civilizations). New York, NY: Rosen Publishing, 2017.

Nelson, Kristen Rajczak. *Ancient Inca Culture* (Spotlight on the Maya, Aztec, and Inca Civilizations). New York, NY: Rosen Publishing, 2017.

Newman, Sandra. *The Inca Empire* (True Books: Ancient Civilizations). New York, NY: Scholastic, 2010.

Niver, Heather Moore. *Ancient Inca Daily Life* (Spotlight on the Maya, Aztec, and Inca Civilizations). New York, NY: Rosen Publishing, 2017.

Quilter, Jeffrey. *The Civilization of the Incas* (The Illustrated History of the Ancient World). New York, NY: Rosen Publishing, 2013.

Sonneborn, Liz. *Pizarro: Conqueror of the Mighty Incas* (Great Explorers of the World). Berkeley Heights, NJ: Enslow Publishers, 2010.

Stuckey, Rachel. *Life Among the Inca* (Ancient Americans). New York, NY: Rosen Publishing, 2017.

Toledo, Daniel. *Francisco Pizarro: Conqueror of the Inca Empire* (Spotlight on Explorers and Colonization). New York, NY: Rosen Publishing, 2017.

BIBLIOGRAPHY

Bingham, Hiram. *Lost City of the Incas.* Phoenix, AZ: Orion Publishing Group, 2003.

Collyns, Dan. "Peru Airs News in Quechua, Indigenous Language of Inca Empire, for First Time." *The Guardian.* December 14, 2016. https://www.theguardian.com/world/2016/dec/14/peru-nuqanchik-quechua-broadcast-inca-empire.

"Colonial Economy." *Discover Peru.* Retrieved May 1, 2017. http://www.discover-peru.org/colonial-economy.

D'Altroy, Terence N. *The Incas.* Hoboken, NJ: Wiley-Blackwell, 2015.

Diamond, Jared. *Guns, Germs, and Steel.* New York, NY: W. W. Norton, 1999.

The Great Inca Rebellion. Written and produced by Graham Townsley, performances by Jay O. Sanders, Guillermo Cock, Elena Goycochea, and Melissa Murphy. NOVA/PBS, 2007.

Hemming, John. *The Conquest of the Incas.* Wilmington, MA: Mariner Books, 2003.

Lane, Kris. "Potosí Mines." *Latin American History: Oxford Research Encyclopedias.* May 2015. http://latinamericanhistory.oxfordre.com/view/10.1093/acrefore/9780199366439.001.0001/acrefore-9780199366439-e-2.

MacQuarrie, Kim. *The Last Days of the Incas.* New York, NY: Simon & Schuster, 2007.

Morris, Craig and Adriana von Hagen. *The Incas.* New York, NY: Thames & Hudson, 2011.

Owen, James. "Lost Inca Gold—Ransom, Riches, and Riddles." *National Geographic.* Retrieved May 1, 2017. http://science.nationalgeographic.com/science/archaeology/lost-inca-gold.

"Peru Church and Religion." CountryReports.org. 2017. http://

www.countryreports.org/country/Peru/religion.htm.

"Peru: Demographics." CountryReports.org. 2017. http://www.countryreports.org/country/Peru/population.htm.

Pringle, Heather. "Inca Empire." *National Geographic.* April 2011. http://ngm.nationalgeographic.com/2011/04/inca-empire/pringle-text.

Quilter, Jeffrey. *Treasures of the Andes: The Glories of Inca and Pre-Columbian South America.* London, UK: Duncan Baird, 2005.

Smith, Bonnie G. *The Oxford Encyclopedia of Women in World History*, vol 1. Oxford, UK: Oxford University Press, 2008.

Tegel, Simeon. "Cerro Rico: The Mountain that Eats Men." *PRI.* March 20, 2013. https://www.pri.org/stories/2013-03-20/cerro-rico-mountain-eats-men.

INDEX

ABOUT THE AUTHOR

Alexis Burling has published dozens of books and articles for kids and teens on a variety of topics ranging from current events and career advice to biographies of famous people. She also specializes in writing riveting accounts of key moments in history. In 2008, she traveled to Machu Picchu for the first time. She found it so interesting that she returned three years later and spent a month traveling around Peru and learning about the Inca civilization. Burling lives with her husband in Portland, Oregon.

PHOTO CREDITS

Cover, (inset) pp. 14, 21, 25, 29, 31 Universal History Archive/Universal Images Group/Getty Images; p. 4 Celso Mollo Photography/Moment Select/Getty Images; pp. 7, 16, 24, 33, 43 pimchawee/Shutterstock .com; p. 9 Peter Groenendijk/Publisher Mix/Getty Images; p. 10 Werner Forman/Universal Images Group/Getty Images; p. 12 Richard Bergmann/Science Source/Getty Images; p. 17, 42 De Agostini/G. Dagli Orti/Getty Images; p. 18 Fototeca Storica Nazionale/Hulton Archive/ Getty Images; p. 26 PHAS/Universal Images Group/Getty Images; p. 34 John Judkin Memorial, Bath, Avon, UK/Bridgeman Images; p. 36 NYPL/Science Source/Getty Images; p. 39 Starcevic/IStock Unreleased/ Getty Images; p. 44 Jacek Kadaj/Moment/Getty Images; p. 47 Bartosz Hadyniak/E+/Getty Images; p. 49 Frank Gaglione/Stone/Getty Images; p. 52 Cris Bouroncle/AFP/Getty Images; back cover, pp. 11, 19, 22, 30, 37, 40, 45, 50-51 rangizzz/Shutterstock.com.

Design: Brian Garvey; Layout: Ellina Litmanovich;

Editor: Amelie von Zumbusch; Photo Researcher: Nicole Baker

A CAREER IN

PAVING AND ROAD SURFACING